Teaching

2 0 1

More Devotions for Christian Teachers

Edward Grube

SAINT LOUIS

For Renee on 25 years in the teaching ministry

Copyright © 1999 Concordia Publishing House
3558 S. Jefferson Avenue, St. Louis, MO 63118-3968
Manufactured in the United States of America

Library of Congress Cataloging-in-Publication Data

Grube, Edward C., 1947-
Teaching 201 : more devotions for Christian teachers / Edward Grube.
p.   cm.
ISBN 0-570-05222-x
1. Christian teachers Prayer-books and devotions—English. I. Title.
II. Title: Teaching two hundred one.
BV4596.T43G78   1999
242′.69—dc21   99-38159

1 2 3 4 5 6 7 8 9 10   08 07 06 05 04 03 02 01 00 99

Contents

Introduction

Dear Teacher,

Teachers never know enough. You probably thirst for adventures in education—new ways to teach, discoveries of new knowledge, publication of innovative books, reviews of prospective curricula, next year's class, next week's lunch menu! Then you spread that enthusiasm around, leaving students smarter because of your efforts.

Teachers never know enough. You also hunger for God's Word—not only for yourself, but also to nurture your students. This book won't directly help your students grow in faith. But as you grow through the Word, you spread more enthusiasm—enthusiasm that truly gives your students something for which to live.

Teachers never know enough. But you already know that. (Or you've heard it before.) It's that appetite for knowledge that drives you to serve God by serving His children. And it's your relationship with Jesus that involves you with Christian education. It's your relationship with Jesus that compels you to include in your spiritual life everything from the most mundane to the marvelously magnificent. May the Holy Spirit ever empower you to teach His Word even as you learn it.

Teaching 201 is a continuation of *Teaching 101*. Each meditation connects God's Word with some facet of your life as a teacher. I hope the meditations also bring you closer to Jesus—you can never get too close—and to the Word by which God speaks to us today.

God bless you, dear teacher.

Edward Grube

Teaching 201

Teaching 201

What a privilege to be a teacher! You build muscles pulling on stubborn boots. Students happily share things with you—leftover snacks, family secrets, the flu. They lavish you with dandelion bouquets or sprays of peonies (ants included). Students fill your life with laughter, treating you to knock-knock jokes and sometimes a few lines they heard dad say over the basement phone. Finally, you go home each night fully confident that some parent will brighten your social life with a call after 9 P.M.

When His family heard about this, they went to take charge of Him, for they said, "He is out of His mind." Mark 3:21

No wonder some people think teachers are, to use biblical language, out of their minds. They might think you're completely over the edge if you teach in a Christian school. Education pays. Unless you teach in a place like that. So why do you teach? The answer is simple. You *are* out of your mind.

You're in good company, though. Jesus' family thought He was "out of His mind" too. In a way, they were right. Jesus was different, and so are you.

God called you to teach. You tell kids about the important things of life—reading, language, math, science, and social studies. But you offer so much more. You share how God's Son suffered and died and rose from the dead to give sinners eternal life. But maybe you should stop there. That kind of talk may earn you what Paul earned before King Agrippa and Festus. " 'You are out of your mind, Paul!' [Festus] shouted. 'Your great learning is driving you insane' " (Acts 26:24).

Much of what Christians teach seems like insanity. Yet you must be bold. You have God's Word supporting what you teach and the Holy Spirit working through that Word to nourish hungry young souls.

As long as you're out of your mind and into your soul, you're really in your right mind. Jesus made you right. He enabled you to teach His Word, and He will give you success. Sometimes. Some will harden their hearts against God's Word. Even Paul had that trouble, but he also had a sane attitude about it. "Agrippa said to Paul, 'Do you think that in such a short time you can persuade me to be a Christian?' Paul replied, 'Short time or long—I pray God that not only you but all who are listening to me today may become what I am, except for these chains' " (Acts 26:28–29).

Prayer

Thank You, Holy Spirit, for taking me from my own mind into the mind of Jesus. Work through all that I teach to take my students there too. In Jesus' name. Amen.

Curriculum Guide 1: History

On the evening of that first day of the week, when the disciples were together with the doors locked for fear of the Jews, Jesus came and stood among them and said, "Peace be with you." *John 20:19*

This is the first in a series of curriculum guide meditations. The subject is history. History should be easy to teach because it repeats itself. Of course, every time it does, the cost doubles. In terms of the classroom, history needs to repeat because the kids probably didn't listen the first time. As you teach history, be aware that the subject has critics who can't agree on what really happened, sort of like witnesses to an accident.

Some people seek to revise history to correct slanted viewpoints, amend weak evidence, or shift blame. This is nothing new. Satan often makes a case against the Christian's history book. He prefers that we question the history of salvation and that we use our God-given intelligence to "see through" what holy men of God wrote for our benefit. Sometimes his plan works. In fact, the history of salvation reports that the devil often succeeds. But his biggest defeat thus far is what makes Christian history such good news.

History records many dark days, but none was darker than that Friday some 2,000 years ago. On this day, three men hung from crosses on a hill outside Jerusalem. History might credit the Jews, in collaboration with the Romans, for the death of the innocent One on the cross, but we need to revise that story a bit. (And the truth hurts!) You and I are responsible. You and I and everyone else who has ever lived and who is yet to live. We sinners deserve to be convicted in a kind of reverse class action suit. Our sinfulness didn't stop God from saving us, however. His love is more potent than our sin.

Today's Bible passage assures us that Jesus rose from the dead. As the apostle Paul later commented, our own resurrection would only be fantasy were it not for Jesus' triumph over the grave. Today's passage is the best of what history offers: eyewitness testimony *and* God's completely believable Word. This is the only history we can thoroughly trust. All others might be as one gentle critic said: "History is gossip that has grown old gracefully." Thank God the real grace isn't just gossip!

Prayer

Thank You, God, for the history of salvation and for making me one of its main characters. Keep me faithful to You, and help me fight any temptation to revise Your story. Amen.

Curriculum Guide 2: Mathematics

Do not add to what I command you and do not subtract from it, but keep the commands of the LORD your God that I give you. *Deuteronomy 4:2*

Your curriculum should include five mathematical operations: add, subtract, multiply, divide, and incomprehensible, as in calculus (or on the elementary level, the metric system). Today's meditation does not concentrate so much on mathematical operations as it does on spiritual operations. Let's examine the first two operations together under the Deuteronomy Property, which is found in our Bible passage.

Sometimes teachers get carried away. In spiritual matters, the operations of adding and subtracting sometimes tempt teachers to alter Scripture. All Law and no Gospel, or vice versa, corrupts God's scriptural equation. Though God's Law seems to cover every conceivable situation, certain circumstances tempt teachers to slip in a few extra commandments or, at least, a flock of consequences and credit God for the additions. On the other hand, kindly teachers sometimes ignore sinful behavior to the extent that their students are in spiritual, if not physical, danger. Strive for good balance in your classroom. Let God's Word, both Law and Gospel, be His word—no more and no less.

Next, we have the operation of division as explained by the John Property: "Thus the people were divided because of Jesus" (John 7:43). Imagine you find a note on your desk. It's from God, and it says, "Proclaim the faith I gave you, but know that not every student will believe. Never stop telling them how much I love them, but you aren't responsible if they won't believe. Some will even cause trouble because of your faith. Discuss it with Paul later."

Finally, the good stuff—multiplication according to the Mark Property: "Still other seed fell on good soil. It came up, grew and produced a crop, multiplying thirty, sixty, or even a hundred times" (Mark 4:8). The Holy Spirit will cause seeds of faith to grow in your students. In turn, the Spirit will work through your students to plant more seeds to grow in faithful followers.

God uses people like you to teach spiritual equations. All things considered, your role as a Christian teacher really adds up.

Prayer

I did the math, Lord. You have subtracted my sin, multiplied my blessings, divided me from the devil, and added immortality to my life. I praise You. Amen.

Curriculum Guide 3: Science

Now faith is being sure of what we hope for and certain of what we do not see.

Hebrews 11:1

Hear a quotation by a faceless scowler, er, scholar. Anonymous defined science this way: "Science is an orderly arrangement of what, at the moment, seems to be facts." As theoretical as science often is, facts are applied to everyday life. One rumor has it that the tobacco and alcohol companies are conducting clandestine research to find an ailment that only smoking and drinking can cure. On other fronts, science has met with mixed success. It puts people in outer space, but it can't keep raccoons out of your garbage.

If you teach science, you have experienced the dilemma caused by scientists who think that everything is a theory except their theories. Thus our contention that God created the world is only a theory—and a false one at that. However, big bangs or dust clouds or enigmatic proteins are theoretically possible! It's enough to make you laugh. Or cry.

Today's Bible verse couldn't be farther from the scientific approach. Science deals with the formation of theories that are proven, disproved, or remain unproven under observable laboratory conditions and procedures. During that process, a whole new vocabulary evolves for kids to memorize from the science book. But faith is different, as the writer to the Hebrews explained.

While scientists peer through microscopes, telescopes, and other less pleasant scopes, Christians see things through a faith scope. Thus you see things that unbelievers and nonbelievers find invisible. What a gift God has given you! As a teacher empowered by the Holy Spirit, you can share your discoveries with the students in your classroom. Just as you might view bacteria through a microscope, you can spot your sins through the eyes of faith. Funny thing, though, when you try to bring up the magnification a few notches, everything disappears. That's because Jesus took away your sins.

Scientists demand proof, evidence that verifies theories or ideas. You might like some too? Look at the cross. It's empty, isn't it? See the tomb? Nothing there either. Seeing is believing. Or is it more like believing is seeing?

Prayer

Lord God, don't let science become a false religion for my students. Instead, help me teach science and every other subject through the eyes of faith. Amen.

Curriculum Guide 4: Social Studies

God did this so that men would seek Him and perhaps reach out for Him and find Him, though He is not far from each one of us.

Acts 17:27

One facet of every social studies curriculum is a book about your community. It's usually an enjoyable book that helps kids study community characteristics. Your students visit the fire department and the police department (on friendly terms). Sometimes you even have a big book or a floor display that colorfully illustrates elements common to most communities.

Your community may have a bank. It's important for kids to know about this institution. Of course, they may have gotten the impression from Mom and Dad that banks are places that dispense money; therefore, they are happy places. Come to think of it, bankers do smile a lot. Students need to know that banks store people's earthly treasures. Spiritual treasures are best kept in the heart where they can do good for others. The wonderful thing about spiritual treasures is the more you spend them, the more you have!

Your community has a city hall. Kids need to know that communities need a fair way to govern people. Otherwise, people would do what they want. Those who work at the city hall often think they can solve all problems by passing laws. That doesn't work any better for government than God's Law did for believers. It wasn't God's fault, though. But He did fix our case by sending Jesus to obey the Law for us and to bring us salvation.

Your big book probably pictures many other community fixtures—groceries, a park, a hospital, the post office, a school, happy people on the sidewalks, and public works employees on break. Check again. Is there a church?

Those who plan social studies books may or may not include a church in their snapshot of a typical community. That's okay. Look at today's passage from Acts. God is everywhere. Tell your students this. Bureaucrats running city hall, desperate loan applicants at the bank, and workers toiling inside and out all need to know that Jesus is close by, even when they're not in church. Isn't it good to know that no matter where you are, God is with you?

Prayer

Help me, Lord, to see You in all of life. Stay close to me, and make Your presence known to all who seek answers to their questions, solutions to their problems, and success in their jobs. Amen.

Curriculum Guide 5: Physical Education

However, I consider my life worth nothing to me, if only I may finish the race and complete the task the Lord Jesus has given to me—the task of testifying to the gospel of God's grace. *Acts 20:24*

One teacher said he practiced physical fitness by walking a mile regularly once each semester. (That's twice as often as those less fit.) If you didn't find that humorous, you're probably among those who take seriously the need for physical fitness. Perhaps you're even a P.E. teacher. At the very least, you can blow a whistle!

Today's Bible passage may not completely satisfy physical fitness advocates, but it does describe earnest and eager Christians. Note that there is no mention of winning, much less free agency or multimillion dollar contracts.

No doubt you run a lot. Teachers are noted for it. Yet you're not part of a race to prove your superiority. Instead, you race to complete all that needs doing to equip your students with the tools of faith. Perhaps a child isn't baptized, and you feel an urgency to help save that child's life. Maybe you hurry to cram in all those last-minute things you want to say in connection with the religion lesson. Or perhaps you have another deadline: Amal is moving, and this may be your last opportunity to expose him to the love of Jesus Christ. Yes, teacher, you run many races.

Your job is to run and that includes running to the cross when sin knocks you down or holds you back. That can be quite a task, especially if you have to take others with you. Not that you drag them to Jesus. Sometimes, however, it takes an all-out sprint to show students the love of Jesus. And you can't rest there. You race back to serve those kids who desire, demand, or even resist nourishment for their faith.

Will you ever rest from this race? Yes. Some may grieve when that day comes, but you will be happy. It will not be the ecstasy of winning the race, but you will be content to have finished. After all, the winner crossed the finish line 2,000 years ago.

Prayer

Keep me in the race, Lord, as I minister to the students under my care. Help me teach them how to run with fleet-footed faith that they, too, may join Jesus in the winner's circle when He shares His victory. Amen.

Curriculum Guide 6: Reading and Writing

Suddenly the fingers of a human hand appeared and wrote on the plaster of the wall, near the lampstand in the royal palace. The king watched the hand as it wrote. ... The king called out for the enchanters, astrologers and diviners to be brought and said to these wise men of Babylon, "Whoever reads this writing and tells me what it means will be clothed in purple and have a gold chain placed around his neck, and he will be made the third highest ruler in the kingdom." *Daniel 5:5, 7*

God doesn't write on walls anymore. He packed His message neatly in a form that anyone can read. Not everyone understands what they read, however. That's where you come in.

As you teach children to read and write, you are blessed with a "Daniel" opportunity to reveal God's Word. Your students will learn enough words to read the Bible. They also will learn how to string letters together for others to read. The Holy Spirit, working through you, will cause something else to happen. The faith He puts in their hearts will enable them to listen to your religion lessons and to read Bible stories so they can see God's hand at work in their lives. When you perceive that process taking place, subjects like reading and handwriting take on what economists call "added value."

To recognize and reveal God's involvement in your students' lives, realize that He is active in your life. Sin sometimes muddles that revelation—sort of smudging God's clear message into unintelligible graffiti. Perhaps that's why God gave us one symbol rather than a string of words to keep His foremost message sharp and well-defined. Just look at the cross. When you're deep in sin, the cross tells you that God's Son died to take away your sins. When guilt collars you and you struggle for escape, the cross rises above you, reminding you to hang your guilt on its crossbeam.

Teach reading and handwriting from your own experiences with the Savior, as well as from the assigned textbooks. Show students the Good News that God wrote for them. The message is a lot better than the one Daniel had to deliver. Who knows? Maybe one of your students will give you something purple. (Probably grape bubble gum.)

Prayer

Thank You, Holy Spirit, for revealing God's love and glory to me. As I teach, help me to show the same to my students. Amen.

Curriculum Guide 7: Assessment

We ought always to thank God for you, brothers, and rightly so, because your faith is growing more and more, and the love every one of you has for each other is increasing.

2 Thessalonians 1:3

You live in the age of the assessment portfolio. Years ago, educators called it something like "I kept some of Albert's papers so you could see why I gave him a *D*." As you can see, education has undergone some positive refinements since the days of the three *Rs* and hickory sticks. The goals have remained constant, though. We want children to grow in knowledge. We want the same for ourselves.

What would your assessment portfolio look like? Hmm. Let's see. Lots of papers. Many suggest that instead of growing, you are slipping backward. Which teacher kept these samples of sin? Ah, it's the devil. That plunges things into perspective. The devil loves to collect evidence of your many failures to learn God's truth. You have to admit that the devil's assessment is accurate. You are awful. As long as you have been immersed in the

Christian faith, you would expect better results. Yet here you are *a sinner*. And you've repeated the grade many times. Not a real plus in the self-esteem department, huh?

The devil is an effective teacher. He's very convincing but odd. First, he teaches you how to sin and how to do it well, then he gives you a failing grade. Sounds like he is a thousand times worse than the worst teacher you can remember! Good thing you have another Teacher. Let's check the portfolio He kept for you.

Looks good, doesn't it? All your work is clean, neat, thorough, and even creative. Upon closer examination of the samples, you recall that you had help with the assignments and tests. Yes, your Father patiently explained what you didn't understand. He kept you focused when your mind wandered. There was discipline, too, but it was loving and in your best interest.

But look. Here's an assignment that doesn't appear to be your work at all. The task was to obtain salvation. You accomplished neither quality nor quantity on your own, so your Brother did the work for you. Some would call that cheating, and in a way, it was. Your Brother beat the devil for you. And it didn't even make your Father angry!

Prayer

Thank You, Jesus, for passing the test that I could only fail. Fill me with Your grace that I may grow more and more. Fill me with love, too, that today's Bible passage might also speak of me. Amen.

Curriculum Guide 8: Music

They sang a new song before the throne and before the four living creatures and the elders. No one could learn the song except the 144,000 who had been redeemed from the earth.

Revelation 14:3

Sidney's music teachers associated him with a musical instrument. They called him a lyre. Okay, so puns about music should be punished by 40 lashes minus one of heavy metal music to the eardrum. Music is serious business! So serious, in fact, that when you enter heaven, if an angel greets you with a harp (a piano after taxes), you can relax. But if he hands you an accordion ...

Music teachers enrich children's lives in ways that some students resist. Discipline problems get up and march to the music. Creative mischief waltzes through their minds, the melody reaching a crescendo about the time the baton points to the principal's office. (*Note*: This is not true of any music teachers actually reading this meditation. Your classes certainly resemble the soothing strains of Saint-Saëns!)

The music of life is often crudely dissonant—globs of notes banging together, defying lyrical rhyme and resonant reason. It's the sound of sin, and sinners like us can hum the cacophony with little effort. Consider the "elevator music" in the courts of Caiaphas and Pontius Pilate and the discordant dirge that accompanied Jesus on the path to Calvary. Some people enjoy that music, but it's really no music at all.

Jesus composed victory music. Leaving the hollow echoes of the grave, He brought jubilant psalms to the lips of His friends. Believers like us have been singing His praises ever since. As today's Bible passage intimates, not everyone knows the song. Perhaps you're trying to teach someone. May God bless that effort! Never be discouraged—God has given you a vast repertoire of grace notes to excite the ears of all who hear. If they refuse to enjoy the music, that's sad, but it's not your fault. So keep singing.

Prayer

Thank You, dear Holy Spirit, for teaching me the words of salvation's song. Help me sing it loudly, and teach it to my students too. Amen.

Curriculum Guide 9: Vocabulary

Then those who feared the LORD talked with each other, and the LORD listened and heard. A scroll of remembrance was written in His presence concerning those who feared the LORD and honored His name.

Malachi 3:16

If vocabulary eschewed multi-syllabic, erudite verbiage, the subject would be called *words*. Funny thing about vocabulary, though, regardless of your vocabulary's limitations, it's always big enough for you to say something you'll regret. Nevertheless, teachers always can work to improve their words, er, vocabulary. If you add a half-dozen new words each month to your vocabulary, you'll soon find that people respect you more. They may not understand you, but you'll wow them with your language! Then again, you may just talk yourself out of a job.

Christianity has its own language. As you teach it to students, you speak words of faith. These words are as normal a part of life for Christians as conversation is for friends. Today's

Bible passage says that as believers talk, God listens in, not as an intruder or judge, but as a third party who blesses our words about Him and each other. He wants us to talk about Him and His family, and He gives us a unique vocabulary for doing so. However, not everyone understands what we say.

If your students have no background in spiritual matters, your vocabulary may be an obstacle. Therefore, it's good to review the elementary words of faith, remembering that you may need to teach their meanings to the children in your class. Two words deserve immediate attention.

1. *Sin.* It's a negative word. Some people consider it a word too dirty even for mouths filled with vulgarity. *Sin* means more than weakness or imperfection. *Sin* is wrongdoing that offends God. *Sin* is behavior that condemns and kills. It litters life with guilt and sadness. *Sin* needs to be removed from sinners.

2. *Grace.* It's more than the name of a table prayer. *Grace* is God's undeserved and unconditional love. God's grace placed Jesus on the cross to take away our sins. His grace saves us and eliminates our guilt. Because of grace, we will live happily every after. That's good news no matter how you say it.

Prayer

Keep me talking, Holy Spirit. "May the words of my mouth and the meditation of my heart be pleasing in Your sight, O Lord, my Rock and my Redeemer" (Psalm 19:14). Amen.

Curriculum Guide 10: Art

Send me therefore, a man skilled to work in gold and silver, bronze and iron, and in purple, crimson and blue yarn, and experienced in the art of engraving, to work in Judah and Jerusalem with my skilled craftsmen, whom my father David provided.

2 Chronicles 2:7

Sometimes teachers in Christian schools must double as art teachers. This can be an ugly subject. Art sits there in the back of the room, taunting the girls, using bad language, defying the teacher ... whoops, wrong Art! The real art is a subject, which come to think of it, often defies teachers too, tempting them to use bad language. No wonder Art sometimes appears as an afterthought in curriculum guides!

The Bible's most notable mention of art is in association with the Old Testament temple. Today's passage suggests images of the decorations adorning Solomon's temple. Much of the art appears to be glimmering mega-jewelry, the kind hung only on the house of the one true God. Impressive as Solomon's Old Testament temple was, the New

Testament changed the image. It pictures Christians as temples. (Thankfully, it doesn't report our dimensions!)

Art takes many forms, and we human temples can assume any of them. Think of yourself as a sculpture for a moment. If you are alone, stand up and shape yourself into a sculpture that personifies your relationship to Jesus. If you're not alone, use your imagination. How would your sculpture be different if you didn't know Jesus? Perhaps you would be nothing more than a molten ball of rusty metal cowering close to the ground.

What if you were an abstract painting? You probably would lose your job, right? Teachers like you need to be more concrete without adopting the characteristics of that rigid-when-set substance. You shouldn't be a still life either. You need to be a picture of energy and activity as you minister to children and their families.

Picture in your mind how a painting of your temple might appear. What role would sin play in your picture? Would you be streaked with sooty, drab colors, or would sin show up in texture and angles? Of course, sin doesn't have to appear at all. Jesus took your sins away and made you a righteous temple. Oh, you need a good cleaning regularly, but it's there for the asking. With that in mind, look at yourself. God is a pretty good artist, isn't He?

Prayer

Thank You, Lord, for decorating my life with love and power. Keep me as clean as a temple and live in me, blessing other people through me. Amen.

Extra Credit

But love your enemies,
do good to them, and
lend to them without
expecting to get anything
back. Then your reward
will be great, and you will
be sons of the Most High,
because He is kind to the
ungrateful and wicked.

Luke 6:35

Occasionally, teachers grant opportunity for students to earn extra credit. This may be the case when hard-working students need a few percentage points to boost a grade that doesn't adequately reflect their effort. At other times, teachers use this tool to keep potentially upset parents away from their telephones. Another use of extra credit is to convince already ideal students that they can exceed 100 percent.

Today's Bible verse refers to extra credit. It's the kind we give, especially to those who don't deserve it. The passage implies that we lavish grace on those we might describe as antagonists. (Okay, sometimes they're more like terrorists.) These are the very people—students, parents, coworkers, etc.—who need our love. To personalize this, think of that one parent who could easily be named Bane of the Year. What could you give him or her, knowing that you will get nothing equally good in return? Remember, we're not talking about professionalism; we're talking about grace.

How about those students who don't like you? Because you are a teacher, you treat them the same as those who do like you. On the other hand, God says that you can do more. You can lavish them with love and mercy and compassion. Sometimes the only thing you can do for such students is pray for them. Only? God has promised to listen to your prayers and act accordingly.

A good way to open your heart for giving extra credit is to remember that you have received a lot of it. Your relationship with Jesus wasn't always this good. There was a time when you didn't believe in Him nor did you want to. In fact, you and Jesus were natural enemies. That's hard to believe now that Jesus not only has credited you with His righteousness, but has called you to serve Him by teaching others. That credit is limitless too. So spend it freely.

Prayer

Dear Jesus, help me to give credit where it's not due. Give me strength through the Holy Spirit to show my love to those who don't love me or even to those who hate me. Thank You for doing the same to me. Amen.

Watch the Back Door

On arriving there, they gathered the church together and reported all that God had done through them, and how He had opened the door of faith to the Gentiles.

Acts 14:27

Congregations often lament "back-door" losses. This term refers to people who join the church but slip away when nobody is watching. Back-door losses are one of the devil's favorites. He doesn't expend much effort as people fall away because of apathy rather than through following more strenuous temptations.

Occasionally, you may find your foot slipping toward that door too. How easy it is to forget God's goodness when things are going well. It's time to keep an eye on that door when you and your class are doing so well that you feel no need for reliance on God. Watch the back door—it's swinging wider.

Paul speaks of no such problem in today's Bible verse. Of course, he also didn't say by which door the new believers entered. As a Christian teacher, the Holy Spirit has used you to make back-door gains for the church as well. Back-door gains are those believers who come to faith when nobody is watching. (Nobody but God, that is.) The only problem with back-door gains is that you may not have opportunity to feel good about your role. Then again, God's New Testament workers didn't worry about that. They always felt good about their work because they knew God would bring success.

You can't plan to gain believers by the back door. It happens as God works through your routine ministry. Day after day, you relate to your children and present God's Word. Both the relationship and the presentation bear fruit. The Holy Spirit works through God's Word and your witness to give your ministry impact that might not be realized for 40 years or more!

God works through you; whether you notice this isn't important. If you were baptized as an infant, you didn't notice when God worked faith in you! The important thing is that He did and He does. Who can say how many you have led to Jesus? God can. He was there. So keep that back door open. It's good to leave the Light on too.

Prayer

Help me, Holy Spirit, to maintain a consistent and robust ministry to my students and their families. I'm not interested in adding notches to my cross. I simply want to serve You and share my faith with others that they may meet their Savior. Amen.

10/05

Adolescents

"The LORD who delivered me from the paw of the lion and the paw of the bear will deliver me from the hand of this Philistine." Saul said to David, "Go, and the LORD be with you."
1 Samuel 17:37

Adolescence is that awkward age when a child is too old to say cute things and too young to say sensible things. Of course, that wasn't the case with David in today's Bible passage. While it sounded as if he were a rebellious youth, David's bravado was fueled by God. The Lord not only had rescue in mind for His people, but He also was setting the stage, or the palace, for the future.

Do you remember your adolescent years? Seems like yesterday, right? Remember the urge to practice your independence? One thing is certain about the adolescent spirit: It shouts, "I can do!"

David would have appreciated the words of Paul who, centuries later, righteously boasted that he could do all things through the power of Jesus Christ. You would fit in well with David and Paul. You also have the power to do God's work, especially as it relates to your classroom. Did you notice the word *practice* in the previous paragraph? Like doctors, like David and Paul, Christianity is a practice.

An old saying goes, "Practice makes perfect." Not so for Christians. Not even for Christian teachers! Sin is a highly effective barrier to attaining what God expects. Sometimes we really are like adolescents, clumsily flopping around as we try to exercise spiritually immature urges. The devil must enjoy a good laugh when he sees us trying harder to be fantastic Christians—without the help of Father, Brother, or Spirit. It's the kind of derisive laughter adults sometimes aim at inept adolescents who are fumbling with failure.

The secret of escaping adolescence is, of course, to depend on God for His divine maintenance plan: Jesus Christ for righteousness and salvation and the Holy Spirit for guarding and building our faith. We also separate ourselves from spiritual adolescence when we study God's Word. Perhaps you already enjoy reading and meditating on Scripture. Through it, God will guide and keep and help you grow to even greater maturity. Talk about growing old gracefully!

Prayer

Lord Jesus, I depend on You for daily forgiveness. Give me a more mature faith and the skills and gifts I need to guide my students too. Amen.

Nothing but Facts

> We did not follow cleverly invented stories when we told you about the power and coming of our Lord Jesus Christ, but we were eyewitnesses of His majesty.
>
> *2 Peter 1:16*

Have you noticed that our federal government fervently forms fact-finding committees to delve mostly into an opposing party's activities? They would do better with less fact-finding and more fact-facing! Too bad the new fitness club in Washington failed. It was dedicated to digging for facts. The legislators were more interested in jumping to conclusions.

We have come to expect cleverly invented stories from those we elect to serve our country. Some individuals have built careers on their ability to fabricate elements of truth around deliberate lies. These spin doctors are members of what is really an old profession.

In Bible times, "spin doctors" served the church of false gods. Or they served a government that had set itself up to be a god. Or in some cases, they served the one who thought whitewashing tombs would give death a better name. Yes, the devil is the father of fraud and deception. Has he worked his spin on you?

The devil makes sin look good. When he tempted the hungry Jesus in the wilderness, he didn't dwell on the misery of a growling stomach. He invited Jesus to a feast; he probably set out a picnic basket, brushed away the ants, and laid out morsels that seduced both taste buds and nostrils. Jesus clung to God's Word and resisted. Would that we had the power just to push away from the bowls and platters at our tables!

Jesus made sin look bad. It was especially hideous when it plastered Him to the cross. Although He died and was buried to take away our sins, He rose from the dead with a promise that the same will happen to us. This was no whitewashed spin on death nor was it a hollow political promise. It was fact! And the fact is that you have eternal life. It began when you came to faith, continues daily through your earthly life, and eventually will reach its climax when you die only to come alive again. Now that's something you can share with your students. They're never too young to learn the facts of life.

Prayer

I thank You, Lord, for giving me the facts. They are so good that they need no fluff! Use me to teach the facts to others. Amen.

Disagreements

> And the Lord's servant must not quarrel; instead, he must be kind to everyone, able to teach, not resentful.
>
> 2 Timothy 2:24

The safest way to disagree is very quietly. After all, not everyone can be as logical, authoritative, informed, confident, and opinionated as you! Disagreement is a customary way of life for some people. They enjoy disagreeing simply for the sake of argument or harassment. Seems like you get at least one parent like that every year, right?

Paul had good advice for young Timothy in today's Bible verse. The advice applies to all Christians, but you, as a teacher, might find it especially helpful. Let's examine the passage more closely.

Paul addresses Timothy as the Lord's servant. Faithful servants remember what they are—servants. Can you imagine a servant lasting long on the job if he repeatedly argues with his master? While you may have a clean record when it comes to arguing with students, parents, or coworkers, you don't do as well with your

Master. Every sin is like a quarrel with Jesus. We easily stray from Him: thinking sinful thoughts, using His name improperly, or simply ignoring His will. Thank God our Master isn't an earthly employer! He forgives and restores our relationship so we may continue serving Him.

It's hard not to quarrel or argue with antagonists, especially students who do not respect us and parents who listen to only their child's story. It's hard to avoid resentment, even after heated words cool. Yet that is the task of God's servants. Perhaps it helps to remember our relationship with Jesus when bitterness or hostility bores into our heart. As His servant, we respond in one way: Treat others as Jesus treats us. And what will be our reward? It might be spite. But as Proverbs says, gentle answers sometimes soften others. One thing is certain, the Lord whom you serve knows the situation and will help you to model your life after His.

You're never alone in testy situations. Jesus is with you. So is the Holy Spirit, who eagerly matches an adversary's adrenaline high with an equalizing flow of peace. So when you want to "let loose" at someone, go ahead. Open the dam to the pool of kindness with which the Spirit fills your servant's heart.

Prayer

Lord Jesus, help me show kindness and restraint. Help me serve You without quarreling or bitterness, and give me an endless supply of forgiveness to heap on others. Amen.

Good Questions

When Jesus entered Jerusalem, the whole city was stirred and asked, "Who is this?"

Matthew 21:10

As an educator, you're not responsible for knowing all the answers, but you better have a stocked arsenal of questions. You learned all about questioning techniques in college. You undoubtedly ask questions of your students that elicit various depths of response, everything from "Huh?" to "The sum of the angles of a triangle is equal to … I forget" to "My mom told me I didn't have to answer that one." You also know (intuitively because they never taught you this in college) the best kind of question to ask friends and apprehensive kids in your class. The best questions are those that they can answer!

Not everyone can answer simple questions. Maybe they expect a trick or, if they're highly educated, they don't believe in simple answers. How do you think Jesus reacted to the question in today's passage from Matthew? Perhaps He wasn't surprised that people didn't know Him. Jesus asked a similar question of the crowds.

Some knew the answer; some hoped they had the right answer; some guessed; others weren't paying attention. Just like English class, huh? (Whoops! Bad questioning strategy. Never ask a yes or no question. The respondent has an automatic 50-50 chance of being right.)

When experiencing your teaching about Jesus, some students may ask, "Who is this?" You understand their wonderment. Who could be born so humbly yet reign so majestically? Who could change water into wine, heal the sick, raise the dead, and withstand the devil's most personal attention? Who could look down from the cross and ask forgiveness for His murderers? Who could love me more than Mom or Dad or Rover? As far as questioning techniques go, these aren't higher-order queries. Good thing too.

A simple answer to the simple question is best for those who ask, "Who is this?" And if you have a simple answer, it's because the Holy Spirit transformed You with the miracle of faith. You may not know all the answers, but you know the most important one. Be sure your students know the answer too.

Prayer

Thank You, Holy Spirit, for telling me the right answer when it comes to questions about Jesus. He is my Savior! Grant me the ability to teach that answer to those whom I serve. Amen.

Oratory Arts

When asked to use the word *oratory* in a sentence, seventh-grader Randi responded, "Some people had to make a choice between being a Whig oratory." She was partly right. Most political types like talking to crowds. The best orators are those who have mastered the art of saying nothing that reveals the fact they have nothing to say. Oratory differs from speech because speech is silver (just as silence is golden), but oratory is all brass.

Jeremiah seems to be a shy person from what we read in today's Bible passage. Then again, maybe not. Would a shy person dare to forestall God? Good thing for believers that God didn't accept Jeremiah's excuse. The reluctant prophet went on to proclaim God's truth under most difficult circumstances. To make matters worse, Jeremiah's problems came more from his own people than from the "enemy"!

God will not accept excuses from you either, not that you would be so brash as to offer any. You may be more like Jeremiah than you think, however. Apparently, Jeremiah was ordinary, at least he thought of himself that way. Maybe that fits your self-assessment. God has a long history of calling common people to do His work. You are part of that history because God has selected you to teach. You don't have to make excuses.

God first equipped you for ministry by taking away your sins. You can't work for Him unless you are spiritually clean and righteous. Not being able to accomplish that yourself, the Spirit gave you faith to rely on Jesus for this cleansing. Now that Jesus has taken away your sins, you can work among your students and colleagues. But God doesn't leave you on your own. He sends the same Spirit who delivered your faith to strengthen you for the work ahead.

You may be neither a Whig oratory. Your words may not be eloquent nor may you consider yourself especially gifted. But God made you a teacher. He gave you a golden opportunity to declare a message more precious than silver, and He will even give you a little brass to accomplish the task.

Prayer

Thank You for making me a teacher, Lord. Give me some of Jeremiah's courage and simple eloquence as I spread Your Word among my students. Amen.

Experience Counts

Jesus ... said, "Go home to your family and tell them how much the Lord has done for you, and how He has had mercy on you." *Mark 5:19*

If you are new to your profession, you can be confident that God has equipped you to begin working. If you have a few years behind you, you have begun to appreciate the benefits of a little experience. If you're close to retirement, you've gained a wealth of experience in time to stop using it!

Let's examine some definitions for *experience*. Experience is

- what teaches you that you need a lot more.
- what causes *deja vu* when you make mistakes.
- what you get when you're expecting something else.
- what helps you make old mistakes in new ways.
- the best teacher. (But oh the tuition!)

Regardless of how many years you have been teaching, you have the most valuable experience. Mark reported the gist of that experience in today's Bible passage when he quoted Jesus. The context of Jesus' command was His healing of a man possessed by a demon. The man was so relieved and grateful that he wanted to follow Jesus. Jesus had a better idea. In effect, Jesus told the man he could follow Him by staying home and sharing his experience with his family.

It's unlikely that you are demon-possessed. However, you are a sinner. The only way to lose those sins is to lay them before Jesus. His forgiveness brings you closer to Him. You may even wish you were with Him right now. Even the apostle Paul had that wish, which he told God about in prayer. Paul also knew that his own desires might be at odds with God's will, so he committed himself to the Lord's work on earth until God took him home. Your school and home are hardly heaven, but you do have a piece of heaven on earth. You have the Gospel. Jesus' words to the man are also His words to you.

Even if you don't teach a religion class, you can apply your experience in the classroom. In words, and especially in actions, you can witness to God's mercy as you have personally experienced it. That personal experience combined with teaching God's Word will generate a positive impact on those you teach. It will give your students an experience they will never forget. Never.

Prayer

Thank You, Lord, for Your love and mercy. Use my experiences through faith to affect an eternal influence on the students I teach. Amen.

Getting Better

In all my prayers for all of you, I always pray with joy because of your partnership in the gospel from the first day until now, being confident of this, that He who began a good work in you will carry it on to completion until the day of Christ Jesus. *Philippians 1:4–6*

Eventually you reach an age when you don't want to look in a mirror (except to see how close that truck is tailgating you). It rarely provides evidence that things are improving. About the only consolation is that the view in the mirror refutes evolutionary theories that fraudulently claim living things improve over time. Mutation is more like it! Well, maybe you don't have that problem.

As you read in the previous devotional, your experience with God's grace and mercy equips you for both teaching and living. Today's Bible selection claims that you're doing quite well. You can even expect to get better because the Holy Spirit will continue to enrich your experience until you retire from God's work.

You know how hard it can be to improve yourself. Whether it's trying to lose weight or gain it, keep your hair looking youthful or simply keeping it, learning a new language or mastering your old one, conquering that new computer program just in time for the upgrade, or trying harder to erase sin from your life, the road to improvement is as long and bumpy as this sentence.

Let's take a closer look at the last improvement: trying harder to erase sin from your life. To put it bluntly, it's impossible. The harder you try to erase sin, the more you'll become frustrated. Worse, you may delude yourself into thinking you are doing well at the task. The good news is that trying harder doesn't work at all, but asking forgiveness does. Jesus freely gives what you ask, and in the process not only takes away your sins, but makes you a partner in His ministry. Talk about a bonus! To make it better, He blesses, maintains, and authorizes you to work for Him until you're done.

Christ's workers are done only when He says they're done. For some it's over at age 5; for others retirement comes at 65 or 95. While using the time granted to you for working in God's earthly kingdom, be assured that the blessed end is in sight. Meanwhile, keep the best teacher's aide busy—with the work He's given you to do!

Prayer

Use me, dear Jesus, to touch the lives of my students, not with my own ideas or prejudices, but with Your Word, forgiveness, and love. Amen.

The Dog (Who Ate Homework)

So I told them, "Whoever has any gold jewelry, take it off." Then they gave me the gold, and I threw it into the fire, and out came this calf!

Exodus 32:24

You probably have collected an extensive archive of excuses during your teaching career. It's unlikely that you could match the one Moses heard in today's Bible reading. It came from Moses' brother as he explained the golden calf. Moses' reaction was a bit more severe than, "Kids say the most amazing things!"

Modern, education-oriented excuses often are variations on the theme, "The dog ate my homework." Variants include, "I set my report card on top of the lamp, but the only damage is where one grade burned out." Or "My father said I didn't have to do it. He's in Australia, but he called long-distance to tell me." Or "We ran out of newspaper for the bird cage." Or ...

The best advice for making excuses is this: If you have one, don't use it. Even if it's a good one, people won't believe you. Precious minutes of life waste away, however, as people endeavor to concoct credible and complex excuses. Perhaps you've dabbled in that exercise yourself. But of course you also know that one thing is better than a good excuse—confession.

How might Old Testament history be different if Aaron had confessed his weak leadership? We can't be too hard on Aaron, though. If he hadn't messed up, someone else would have. In fact, if you examine the last few days, perhaps there were times when you abandoned God's Law or Gospel in favor of allowing the dog to eat it. (Or even feeding it to him.)

Instead of creativity, you need to deal honestly with sin, confessing it to Jesus in full confidence that He will forgive. Once forgiven, you are free to forgive and to teach your students that they need not make excuses. Assure them that they can approach you with the same confidence that you feel when approaching your Savior. On the cross, Jesus eliminated the need for excuses. So tie up that dog! Turn off that lightbulb. Don't answer the phone if it's your father calling from Australia. Make your excuses *ex*-cuses.

Prayer

Dear Jesus, I confess that I have sinned. I have no excuse. I need forgiveness. I need the power to fight temptation. I pray in Your name. Amen.

Training Wheels

The fastest way to learn to ride a bicycle is to use training wheels. Back in the '50s, when training wheels were found only in suburbs, many children learned to balance on two wheels in a city alley. No studies exist to prove it, but alley riders probably learned quicker than training wheelers. After all city alleys are receptacles for garbage, broken bottles, and dog-walking leavings. The fear of falling kept bike-riding novices in better balance than training wheels. You didn't want to lean toward the pavement!

Many parents would read today's passage from Proverbs and cross-stitch it on a plaque—as a Christmas present for you! The truth, as you know so well, is that parents have prime responsibility for raising children and for helping them grow in Christ. What did people do before the advent of schools? They did what God intended. But as sin snaked its way from the garden to the globe, circumstances changed the way people lived. Economies developed that improved lives in some ways but demeaned them in others. Developing economies and complex educational needs were married and a new need sprang up for their offspring—schools.

Do you realize that the environment you provide at school and church is more stable than many children have at home? Parents burdened with debt, demanding careers (or unemployment), dysfunctional relationships, and other evils often entrust their children to you. These parents hope that you will become even more than *in loco parentis.* How is it that parents can trust you?

You have the model Father. From Him, you have learned forgiveness, justice, compassion, and wisdom. You have learned these things firsthand! How God has blessed you, a poor and miserable sinner. Now you're what every parent can be. You're a saint. As saint, you know the love of Jesus and want to train others in it. May God never let you depart from that. This is one place you don't want to fall!

Prayer

‣ My students need parents, Lord. Bless theirs that they may fulfill the God-given responsibilities of parenthood. Bless me, too, that I may be a partner in the privilege of raising Your children. Amen.

What?

So Eli told Samuel, "Go and lie down, and if He calls you, say, 'Speak, LORD, for your servant is listening.' " So Samuel went and lay down in his place.

1 Samuel 3:9

God truly used His unfathomable wisdom to create everything. Look at the human body. (Well, maybe someone else's!) Miles of tubing weaves throughout the body, linking living cells with lifeblood. Muscles work when we want them to, unless they're the muscles that sustain life. Then they work automatically. Consider your senses and how they foster enjoyment and safety. The face alone is a miracle. Isn't it wonderful how God made your ears so they wouldn't shut and your mouth so it will?

Listening is an art. Some of your best classroom listeners give their complete attention without a hint that they haven't absorbed a word! Others are fighting dragons with their rulers or rummaging through their desks. You're positive they aren't paying attention. Or are they? Most kids need a little help to become effective listeners. Like Samuel, they need some guidance. Once Samuel listened, it transformed his life.

How are you at listening? One measure of teaching prowess is to assess the ratio of teacher talk to student talk. Dynamic classrooms have lots of student talk; either that, or the teacher has a sore throat! Good listening also facilitates good relationships with students' families. The best listening, however, happens when you can hear what isn't being said.

Have you listened to God lately? Isn't it as if He actually speaks to you when you confess your sins and He forgives you? How else would you know you are forgiven unless you heard it from Him?

God spoke His words long ago, and they were recorded by those He commissioned to pen the Bible's words. When you read the Bible, you hear God. You hear Him tell how He created the world. You hear Him tell how you're a sinner in a very long line of sinners that reaches back to the first people on earth. You hear His promises of a Savior and listen as He urges His people through the voices of prophets. Then you hear the best news. Oh, the setting is frightening, but you hear Jesus exclaim from the cross, "It is finished." What better words have you ever heard?

Prayer

Dear God, thank You for speaking to me. Make me a good listener. Amen.

Blue Genes

Surely I was sinful at birth, sinful from the time my mother conceived me. *Psalm 51:5*

Heredity is what you got from your mother. On the other hand, your father transmitted "hisedity." Now you can tell why this book failed scientific review. (Quit groaning. You haven't stopped since the last bad joke.) The truth is heredity is fascinating. Parents with smart or handsome children firmly believe in heredity, while others less blessed look at each other and wonder.

We like some of the things passed down from our ancestors; others we could do without. One of those "others" is sin. Every generation of every family has this sin—a blue gene that brings sadness and suffering into every life. Some have called this hereditary sinfulness original sin. Nobody escapes it, though some deny its existence and tenaciously insist that innocence is a condition at birth. Psalm 51 clearly refutes this view.

Surprisingly, original or inherited sin supplies a popular crutch. Why worry about living according to God's will if you're sinful even before birth? How serious can original sin be if it's not something you actually do? Ignore it. Let the theologians discuss it.

But original sin is the defect that makes life on earth far inferior to life in heaven. Original sin is what automatically separates us from God. Yet were God to eliminate original sin, the human condition would remain otherwise unchanged. How freely sin originates within us! We need not despair nor lie about our condition. God freely forgives and provides something else to inherit—eternal life.

Discuss genetics with your students. Talk about how they have their dad's hair (now he knows where it went!) or their mom's eyes (especially when they look at themselves). Let them know they have Adam and Eve's sin underneath their own. Be certain to tell them how they also have inherited a life that will never end. They got that from their Father in heaven.

Prayer

Dear Father, thank You for making me part of Your family. I know You have forgiven my sins, original and personal. Amen.

Popularity Contest

So many gathered that there was no room left, not even outside the door, and He preached the word to them.

Mark 2:2

Your school might conduct spelling bees, fine arts competitions, and athletic games. Parents condone contests such as these, but what would happen if you held a popularity contest? You could be sure you would place last! (Sort of like judging who makes the cheerleading squad.) Popularity isn't everything, however. Look at what the popularity of beef did to cows!

To some, Jesus was popular. To others, He was infamous. Today's Bible passage reports a highpoint in Jesus' earthly ministry. Crowds loved to hear Him preach because He told the truth about their relationship with God the Father. The truth stung them with guilt until Jesus got to the part about forgiveness, free and unobtainable in any other way except through Him. Like us, they didn't completely understand why God would love them as He did. They marveled at the mystery of some of Jesus' remarks. But they understood the way into God's kingdom, which bothered some in the crowd.

People enjoy feeling that they have accomplished something. That's how it was with Jesus' enemies. To them, He was infamous, even blasphemous! Not only did He claim to be God, but He asserted that the highest men of the church were sinners. (Actually, not being concerned with political correctness, Jesus called them vipers.) So incensed were these men that they succeeded in hanging the world's most popular Man on a cross. They also succeeded in fulfilling God's promises.

How do you feel about Jesus? Would He win a popularity contest in your classroom? If you point out the sins of your students without assuring them of forgiveness, Jesus will not be popular. He might not be popular to some regardless of how you portray Him. The hearts of these individuals are still hardened. The best way to help Jesus maintain popularity is to bring Him to all the parties, to recess and athletic contests, to the lunchroom, and to the math class. As children grow in their relationship with Jesus, He will become someone with whom they want to be, especially because they are sinners.

Prayer

Dear Savior, You are popular with me. I want to be with You always. Help me find ways to boost Your popularity among my students too. Amen.

Banquets

He has taken me to the banquet hall, and His banner over me is love.

Song of Songs 2:4

Banquets have become a norm for most schools. Families, students, and faculty attend events, such as the graduation banquet, the sports awards banquet, the scholars banquet, and the recess *cum laude* banquet. Most of these banquets share common elements, including a catered food buffet featuring chicken with a fancy name, potatoes with a fancy name, and slices of cardboard cake supreme (which has a name it deserves). Aside from the food, banquets often conclude with more after-dinner speakers than after-dinner listeners!

Song of Songs mentions a different kind of banquet. It reminds us of the intended nature of banquets rather than the perfunctory gatherings we attend by virtue of our earthly status. You can imagine what any banquet run by Solomon would have been like. No Uncle Monty's Buffet here! No Chicken Pistachio *a la* Rochester either. It's the kind of banquet to which believers will be invited in heaven. With one difference.

Those attending Christ's banquet will be a more diverse group than you would expect at a royal feast or even the sports awards banquet. Jesus said, "But when you give a banquet, invite the poor, the crippled, the lame, the blind" (Luke 14:13). (In some ways, it *does* sound like the sports awards group!)

Our Savior has two criteria for issuing invitations to His banquet. The first is that you must be fit to enter the banquet hall. Put succinctly, you must be perfect. That's not a problem. Jesus made you perfect when He took your sins to the cross. The second thing you need is faith. It can be great or small. It may have accomplished much in His kingdom or it may have succeeded mostly in personal survival. Seating will not be selective. Everyone except the Host had sinner status on earth, which has become sainthood in heaven.

Picture the banquet hall for a moment. It's huge and beautiful—better than anything Solomon's interior decorator ever created. (And Solomon would agree. Just ask him.) The music is angelic and the lighting divine. And look at the heart-shaped banners hanging overhead. One has your name on it.

Prayer

I look forward to Your banquet, Lord Jesus. Thank You for bringing me to the table. I'd like to bring my students along too. Amen.

Computer Literacy

He said to them, "Go into all the world and preach the good news to all creation."

Mark 16:15

Computers have changed the world, though education was a little slow to jump on the mother board. Now, of course, a school isn't considered good unless it enrolls as many computers as students.

As a teacher, you should know the latest developments in computer hardware. First, there's the specially enhanced Administrator Computer. You don't ask it anything, but it tells you anyway. Second, there's the Almost-Human Computer. It recognizes voices and communicates the same. The only bug is that it blames other computers for its mistakes. Last, there's the Apple Polisher Computer. Tell it a joke, and it always laughs. (It's currently on back order.)

If your school facilitates computer literacy, you already know about word processing, spread sheets, and databases. In fact, you may know almost as much as your hard drive. Computer applications are limited only by your imagination. So imagine how you would interface today's Bible passage with computers.

From the outset, let's get beyond Bible software and games based on Bible stories. The computer has as much potential to propagate the Gospel as any communication tool. The printing press put the Bible into the hands and hearts of common people. The computer can send it virtually anywhere serviced by electricity and telephone—not exactly "all the world" but close.

People give much attention to misuse of computer resources such as the Internet. But the web is no different than a bookstore. Or the world. We sinners have found ways to misuse God's gifts ranging from atomic energy to vocal chords, yet He continues to shower us with blessings that have potential to give Him glory. Explore with your class ways to use the computer to fulfill Jesus' command in Mark.

The computer has replaced workers throughout industry, but it will neither replace Jesus nor Christians. Unlike computers, we humans choose to sin, and we need forgiveness. Only Jesus meets our need for pardon. Sinners around the world need forgiveness. Some don't know it, or they refuse to believe. The computer-literate Christian has opportunities to reach these people.

Prayer

Heavenly Father, help me use the resources You have given me to serve You better and to glorify You. Especially, Father, give me ideas on new ways to share the Gospel. (Bless my old ways too.) Amen.

Rainy-Day Resources

Be glad, O people of
Zion, rejoice in the
LORD your God, for He
has given you the
autumn rains in righ-
teousness. He sends
you abundant showers,
both autumn and
spring rains, as before.
Joel 2:23

Good thing Joel wasn't speaking at a teachers' conference. The attendees might have made him stay in from recess on a nice day! Most teachers consider rain at recess a diabolical curse rather than a bounteous bless- ing. If you adopt a spiritually optimistic outlook on life, how- ever, many of the things you consider to be blights actually can be blessings.

One of your major irrita- tions is the disruptive student. Quality is directly associated with quantity here. The more disruptive students in a class, the better they become at their favorite antics. Your ministry to them frequently suffers because they anger and frustrate you. You wish they were in someone else's class, and you would pass them on at the end of the year, even if they needed help suc- cessfully accomplishing recess. Jesus faced peo- ple like this. (Some were even possessed, but don't make comparisons with you-know-who!) Jesus dealt firmly with disruptive people, sometimes even expressing righteous anger. Jesus never stopped loving these people, though, or praying for them. He even prayed as He hung on the cross.

You might remember your own school days somewhat ruefully. Maybe you were one of those irritating students. If not, you still have experience. Despite God's love and care, you remain disruptive. A day doesn't pass when you don't sin. Like most disobedient and bothersome students, you are present in God's kingdom every day. He probably gets angry, but because of Jesus, God's anger never overshadows His compassion and forgiveness. While the devil gleefully puts your name on the left side of the board (so there's lots of room for check marks), Jesus stands with eraser in hand—the eraser His Father gave Him when He graduated from Calvary and the tomb.

Next time it rains at recess, don't be disappointed. Think of it as an opportunity to bond more closely with your class. Perhaps you can get to know better those students whom you aren't anxious to know. Tack on an extra 15 minutes to the next nice-day recess!

Prayer

Help me see Your blessings even in difficult situations, Lord. Help me to think of ways to turn what I don't like into something You like. Amen.

Rare Genius

For God, who said, "Let light shine out of darkness," made His light shine in our hearts to give us the light of the knowledge of the glory of God in the face of Christ. *2 Corinthians 4:6*

Educators have largely abandoned the word that once set apart a single individual in the classroom, the one you wanted to sit behind, especially at test time. Often, it was the individual you didn't want to be near the rest of the day. Fortunately, most of us have avoided taunts of "genius." Even the truest genius has limits, though; too bad that's not true of stupidity!

How do you describe the characteristics of your best and brightest students? Those who are true honor students probably possess more honor than just their grades. You probably know a few straight *A* students, however, who possess poor judgment or can't apply what they have learned. And you're equally familiar with children who struggle for a *C* but can apply everything they learn to some useful purpose.

Perhaps it's good that "genius" is rare—at least in our vocabulary. God certainly would look for different scores than an educational psychologist. In fact, God would find everyone well short of genius proportions and heavily weighted with spiritual stupidity. That's the condition of sinners. Each of us neatly fits that category too. God doesn't leave us without help, though.

The Holy Spirit is like a special tutor, with one major difference. We have no innate spiritual intelligence with which to work. The Spirit takes us from vegetable to genius, and He does it by shining a Light into our hearts. That Light is the one of whom Paul speaks in today's Bible passage—our Savior, Jesus Christ. Our genius is nothing less than a miracle.

Some people would bristle at the suggestion of their hopelessness and helplessness—their complete lack of ability. But you don't have to feel that way. The Spirit made you a true spiritual genius. You know everything you need to know for salvation.

Prayer

Thank You, dear Spirit, for giving me faith in Jesus Christ. Help me grow in that faith and teach me to apply it to everyday life. Amen.

Memorable Quotations

If someone is caught in a sin, you who are spiritual should restore him gently. But watch yourself, or you also may be tempted.

Galatians 6:1

Just like television, this book offers a 10-segment mini-series. This one features the sayings of the previously and frequently cited quote-maker, Anonymous. He or she is a favorite of many people if only because you don't need to worry about misspelling the name. The first quotation is on the subject of charity: "Charity is a virtue, not an organization."

Discuss charity with your class and students are likely to think of money. Children often respond well with their dollars to help the less fortunate. But charity goes beyond currency, as today's Bible verse from Paul counsels. To paraphrase dear old Anonymous: "Charity is an attitude, not a donation."

Your education as a teacher would be incomplete if you didn't master some disciplinary skills. Visit a bookstore and you'll find at least one shelf dedicated to discipline strategies or systems. Surprisingly, most will work if you follow them verbatim and with consistency. But no disciplinary structure is complete if it ignores Galatians 6:1. (By the way, if it worked for God, it will work for those who serve Him too.)

The key to God's success in disciplining His children (no age limit) lies in the phrase "restore him gently." That's exactly what God did for sinners through His Son. As a sinner, others might expect you to fear God in the most negative sense. But you know that God's admonition to charity started at home. His home. He extended that charity to you, not simply ignoring sin and letting you continue it. Nor does He remove the consequences of sin from your earthly life. He does forgive sin freely for Jesus' sake, and that act restores your relationship with Him.

Because you have personal experience with God's disciplinary system, you can apply it to your students. Consistency remains necessary. So does your reliance on the power to forgive from the One who forgave you. So the next time you have a problem in the classroom, be gentle.

Prayer

Lord Jesus, thank You for restoring my broken relationship with You. As opportunities arise, help me practice the same charity toward my students. Amen.

Morality

In my integrity You uphold me and set me in Your presence forever.

Psalm 41:12

On the topic of morality, Anonymous had this to say: "Morals without religion will wither and die, like seed sown upon stony ground or among thorns."

A majority of parents want their children to be moral. Of course, these parents also may discount the negative effects that practices—such as live-in companions, gambling, drinking, and watching smutty TV channels—have on children. What morality really means is not robbing old people, puttering with promiscuity, shooting up the neighborhood or their arms, or otherwise getting their names in the newspaper.

The psalmist used the word *integrity* in place of morality. Is it a more godly word? Probably not. *Integrity* implies wisdom in making life choices. Neither *integrity* nor *morality* carry meaningful impact without faith. Without faith, integrity or morality is what Isaiah called "filthy rags." True integrity is blessed by God for the sake of His Son. It's powered by the Holy Spirit, who enables Christians to live moral lives.

While it's clear where moralistic living originates, the concept of morality can cause difficulty for Christians. Some Christians place more emphasis on morality than they do on the Gospel. By minimizing the source of integrity, they risk taking credit for their moral lives. All people let their morals slip occasionally. Actually, more than occasionally. When that happens, those who think they can attain morality on their own become overcome by guilt or grief. But you know better. When morality falters, only one thing needs to happen: repentance.

When you find your morals lacking, let the guilt drive you to Jesus' mercy. Leave your sins and your guilt at the foot of the cross, and in repentance return to a life punctuated by integrity. The Spirit will help you not only to live morally, but to model those morals for the students in your classroom. You may be the only one who ever models God-given morality to them. Help them realize that morality is a relative term, and the relative is their Brother.

Prayer

Dear Lord, give me wisdom, integrity, and morality as I live my life in Your name. Keep me ever in Your care and guide me to righteous living. Amen.

Fine Food

When Your words came, I ate them; they were my joy and my heart's delight for I bear Your name, O Lord God Almighty.

Jeremiah 15:16

Anonymous may not have wanted credit, but this sounds so good: "Many things in the Bible I cannot understand; many things in the Bible I only think I understand; but there are many things in the Bible I cannot misunderstand." A little long-winded for Anonymous, but oh so true! The Bible offers fine food, and it's good for more than thought. Jeremiah thought God's Word was sweet enough to eat. The reason it's so sweet is because our sins are so sour.

In the welcome quiet at the end of a school day, sit in your chair and survey the empty desks of your students. Think of how you dealt with each one today. Did any sinfulness infiltrate your relationship with them? Think about your thoughts. Regardless of how professional you are, your thoughts may lag behind your deeds. It's a common problem among teachers—even Christian teachers. What about the effort you put into your lessons? Was anything lacking? If not, what about yesterday or last week?

This is not a meditation to make teachers feel rotten, but it will make you a better teacher. It will make you better only if you do something about your weak points. If you had methodology problems, you might consult a methods textbook. If content was deficient, you could learn more at the library or over the Internet. But if sin is your problem, your choices are blessedly limited. You need the Bible.

It's one thing to teach the Bible to children and quite another to educate yourself through it. You need the sweetness of God's Word for forgiveness, comfort, encouragement, and relief. You need it to improve your ministry, growing closer to Jesus and to others. The Bible "pulls no punches" about sin, but it's also frank about forgiveness.

Other books eventually become outdated, but the Bible has been the Christian's reliable text for thousands of years. As the prophet said, "The grass withers and the flowers fall, but the word of our God stands forever" (Isaiah 40:8). Without preservatives!

Prayer

Thank You, Lord, for the Bible. As I read and study it, help me to understand what is necessary to serve You better in my ministry. Amen.

The Angels Win

Are not all angels min-
istering spirits sent to
serve those who will
inherit salvation?

Hebrews 1:14

Anonymous had nothing to say about angels. (He probably was a fan of the Giants.) However, another famous person, John Milton (Anonymous' cousin?), observed that millions of invisible spiritual creatures roamed the earth continuously. Undoubtedly looking for those in trouble, at least according to today's Bible verse.

Milton didn't actually observe angels because they are invisible. But the Bible reveals angels to those who look for them through the eyes of faith. Not long ago, the media focused on angels, including a successful television series and the cover of *Time* magazine. As you recall these events, perhaps it strikes you as strange that people need to see angels to enjoy them. Naturally, a television program with no visible characters wouldn't last beyond the first commercial, but making angels look like humans? Do you think any angels were offended?

Angels are real. On rare occasions, they have appeared to people, including to Mary and Joseph. You don't need to see angels to confirm their existence. The Bible tells us an amazing thing about these heavenly residents. Although they are heavenly beings, they are here to serve us! Did you get that? Serve *us*! Don't bother to look, but angels are likely to visit your classroom regularly. And they're on recess and supervision duty with you. These angels aren't only for children; you have them watching you too.

We might more easily perceive angels' work when we escape danger in some "close call," but who can say that angels don't keep the close call from even coming close? Thank God for angels. They care for you and your students day and night. With God's angels, you never have to worry. They always win.

Prayer

Dear Father, thank You for making angels and sending them to serve me. Send them to protect my students too. Amen.

Hurting Till It Gives

No discipline seems pleasant at the time, but painful. Later on, however, it produces a harvest of righteousness and peace for those who have been trained by it.

Hebrews 12:11

Anonymous knew about affliction. A poetic moment yielded this result: "Come then, affliction, if my Father wills, and be my frowning friend. A friend that frowns is better than a smiling enemy." But, you say, the Bible passage speaks of *discipline*. Are discipline and affliction the same?

Let's frame that question within the context of a classroom like yours. Merton hasn't done his homework for the three years he's been in your classroom. You resolutely decide to do something about it before he's old enough to drive. You make him stay after school until he catches up or you retire, whichever comes first. Merton doesn't like staying after school. It keeps him from watching the afternoon reruns. Worse, he must actually work while he's serving detention. Is he afflicted? He thinks so. Is he experiencing discipline? Certainly!

Who is really responsible for affliction? Often, it's the devil. He enjoys hurting people in hopes that they will curse God or at least forget His existence. Sin afflicts sinners, which is logical and natural. We bring this affliction on ourselves. But God can use affliction to discipline sinners into running to Jesus for help. For some people, that's the only time they snuggle up to Jesus. In that case, discipline (and the affliction) is a lifesaving blessing.

You couldn't teach without discipline in your classroom. You couldn't learn without the Master Teacher's discipline in your life. Think about it. An affliction may discipline you to turn to God. It may send you crashing to your knees in prayer. Think of affliction and discipline as things that hurt "till they give," till they give you a push toward God and His divine relief.

Prayer

I don't like to suffer, Lord. When I do, show me how You are at work in my life. Remind me that You are the one on whom I can rely for help. Amen.

Nothing but the Truth

Anonymous usually tells the truth, sometimes even in rhyme.

> What a shaking thing
> The truth can be,
> Especially when found
> On the family tree.

Did you detect a little sarcasm in that poem? It's probably referring to your spouse's side of the family! Of course, you need look no farther than yourself for some quivering twigs on the family tree.

Jesus answered, "I am the way and the truth and the life. No one comes to the Father except through Me."

John 14:6

It's no news anymore, but the truth is that you are a sinner. (Just ask your students—they may know some of the specifics!) Even if your branch of the family tree looks healthy, you know where your most private sins nest. That's a truth that hurts. But it's not the truth that Jesus talked about in today's Bible verse. He mixed three characteristics of His divinity into one very welcome truth.

The truth is that Jesus saved sinners. He didn't save them in any easy way, either. Suffering abuse from soldiers and from His own people, Jesus went to the cross. There He suffered separation from His Father and physical death. But the truth didn't end there. Jesus rose from the dead. Salvation comes as a result of faith—believing what the Bible and the Holy Spirit claim as truth.

In your ministry to children, you may experience skeptics who claim the Bible is a lie. (Yes, some of those people go to Christian schools.) Of course, you will not give in. It's equally important, however, that you profess the truth gently and clearly. Lives are at stake. Skeptics and unbelievers don't know the way; therefore, their lives are doomed. They may not want to hear you. In extreme cases, they may even flee the truth by taking their children from your school. (And they will blame you!) If that happens, Satan is certain to tweak your guilt-strings. But tell him to go tweak a pitchfork instead. You know the truth, and the truth has freed you from the devil and his accusations.

Prayer

Your truth, Lord, has saved my life. Help me tell the truth to all those You've sent to me. By the power of the Holy Spirit, help them believe it. Amen.

What a Pity!

> Jesus had compassion on them and touched their eyes. Immediately they received their sight and followed Him.
>
> *Matthew 20:34*

As good a creator of quotes as Anonymous was (let's call him by the name his friends use: Anon.), he didn't always spell well. He couldn't spell *good* either! He often mistook the word for a proper name and used an uppercase *G* and dropped an *o*. He tussled with piety too. He often omitted the *e*. When brought to his attention, Anon wasn't concerned. He maintained that the symbolic differences were minimal, if indeed they existed at all!

Jesus' ministry was one of pity and compassion. But as today's Bible passage relates, His love for people went beyond physical healing. Even the blind ended up seeing that which some sighted people couldn't. They saw Jesus as their Savior.

All people are spiritually blind at birth. Sadly, some stay that way. Because God took pity on sinners, He sent His compassionate Son to remove the blindness. He also sent the Holy Spirit to grant the sight of faith. Your first glimpse of Jesus may not have been as spectacular as we read today. If you were baptized as an infant, you probably don't remember much at all. But just as your young eyes began to focus on Mom and Dad, the Holy Spirit showed you your heavenly Father and divine Brother. What a miracle. If you came to faith later in life, perhaps it was like slipping on a pair of glasses—you saw things you never realized were there.

Now it's your turn to bring sight to the blind. The Holy Spirit has appointed you to a ministry that proclaims the Gospel to students. Some in your classes can see; others remain blind. Nurture all your students with God's Word, and heap your compassion on each one. Take special pity on the blind. Touch their darkened eyes with the light of what you know about God and His love for sinners. By the power of the Spirit, they, too, may see Jesus and follow Him.

Prayer

Help me, Lord, to bring the cure for blindness to those who can't see Your Son. Through the power of the Holy Spirit, make me an effective witness to those who haven't seen You and who have seen You. May their vision become sharper as I minister to them. Amen.

You Hypocrite!

The Spirit clearly says that in later times some will abandon the faith and follow deceiving spirits and things taught by demons. Such teachings come through hypocritical liars, whose consciences have been seared as with a hot iron. *1 Timothy 4:1–2*

Are you? Anon said that hypocrites are people who aren't themselves on Sundays. Most Christians are hypersensitive to that word *hypocrite*. In fact, most Christians are hard-pressed to defend themselves against the criticism. Perhaps you have fallen victim to the taunt as students, or their parents, used the word against you. It sometimes seems that the longer one lives as a Christian, the more one is susceptible to accusations of hypocrisy.

So are you? Upon self-examination, you have to admit that you are not always "the person you are on Sundays." You lose your spats with Satan and your own human nature, falling in line with their bidding. Their allure draws you away from the One whom you worship on Sundays. At times, you act as if you don't know Him. But is that hypocrisy? The devil would like you to believe that it is. Perhaps he can use it to drive you from the Savior in a fit of hopelessness, despair, and resignation.

Reread today's Bible selection. If you fear that it applies to you, think again. No, you're not perfect. Occasionally you do exhibit symptoms of hypocrisy. But they are just symptoms brought on by your lack of immunity to sin. Although you are a forgiven sinner, you still sin. Through salvation earned by Jesus and by the power of the Holy Spirit, however, you do not fit the description in Timothy. Because you have real faith, your conscience isn't smoldering in ruins. You haven't abandoned faith nor gleefully danced after demons. Christians aren't hypocrites. Their remnants of sinfulness may suggest otherwise, but God's forgiveness covers that.

Arm yourself against venomous accusations of hypocrisy. Ask the Spirit to guide you to avoid those things that might cause others to call you a hypocrite.

Prayer

Thank You, dear God, for faith. Help me to act in ways that do not invite criticism, and give me strength to endure false accusations. Help me to hate sin as I look forward to that day when I will sin no more. Amen.

2/06

Discipleship

He replied, "I saw Satan fall like lightning from heaven. I have given you authority to trample on snakes and scorpions and to overcome all the power of the enemy; nothing will harm you. However, do not rejoice that the spirits submit to you, but rejoice that your names are written in heaven." *Luke 10:18–20*

A fourth-grade teacher asked his students to define *discipleship*. One girl answered, "It's the boat that almost sank because they caught too many fish." What is your definition? Do you think of how you serve God? Are you like the 72 disciples in today's Bible reading? They had a great time after God commissioned them and they successfully practiced their discipleship. You can almost hear Jesus laugh as He works through you to nurture a student's faith and Satan takes another tumble.

It certainly isn't sinful to enjoy the results of discipleship. But disciples sometimes become preoccupied with what they are doing. In a way, they fill their boat to the point of sinking from their own success. Sometimes they become like the Sons of Thunder, who wanted to fling God's wrath at a town that refused to welcome Jesus. Recognizing that danger, Jesus offered His directive in today's Bible verse. Our wise friend Anon agreed. He said, "We may be doing Jesus an injustice in stressing the fact that He so frequently said 'Go!' His first word to His disciples was not 'go', but 'come.' "

Jesus also invited you to come. By the grace of God, the justification of Jesus, and the strength of the Spirit, you are a disciple. Therefore, you are powerful. Using that Spirit-driven power, you knock Satan around every time you reach a student's heart with your model and message of God's love through Jesus Christ. Yet your greatest delight is that you personally believe that Jesus saved you. You live confidently, sure of the future, knowing that God chose you to be saved, even as He chose you to work for Him.

Use the power of your discipleship as you cruise through life. Always remember that it floats on God's mercy and grace and that it sails on the breath of the Holy Spirit.

Prayer

Dear God, thank You for bringing me into Your family. Thank You, Jesus, for telling me to go. Make me an effective disciple as I await that day when Satan takes his final flop. Amen.

Good Conscience

Now this is our boast:
Our conscience testi-
fies that we have con-
ducted ourselves in the
world, and especially
in our relations with
you, in the holiness
and sincerity that are
from God. We have
done so not according
to worldly wisdom but
according to God's
grace.

2 Corinthians 1:12

Why do writers so often portray *conscience* as a nag? Perhaps it has a negative image because it often treats us like a horse, always saying, "Nay!" How would you describe *conscience*?

In our final quote from Anon, we find this: "It is a beautiful idea that every man has within a Guardian Angel; and it is true too, for Conscience is ever on the watch, ever ready to warn us of danger." Now there's a good description of conscience! It's a guardian angel. In that respect, old cartoons used a good illustration for conscience. You saw an angel over one shoulder and a devil over the other, each urging the main character to action.

The devil wages persistent war over us. Picturing our conscience as a guardian angel reminds us that God's gift of a conscience works to our benefit because of faith. Do all people have a conscience? We can believe that because the apostle Paul tells us that God's Law lives in all humans, regardless of whether they believe in Him. As we believers sin, our conscience reminds us that we have done wrong. The Holy Spirit counsels us to seek God's forgiveness. Conscience helps us distinguish between God's will and our won't.

Conscience is a blessing. The rap it gets for keeping us from trouble is well-deserved. Because we consider conscience within the context of faith, it has a good rap. Not that we always appreciate it when certain sins seem especially appealing! But even in those times, our Guardian Angel is at work. Actually He's at war with the devil to keep us from falling. Thank God for His grace in giving us a conscience. Because God is at work through our conscience, we can value the old maxim: "Let your conscience be your ..."

Prayer

Thank You, Father, for the angels You send to protect me. Thank You also for my conscience. Send Your Holy Spirit to guide me in the way I should go. Amen.

On Being Choosy

You make many choices as a teacher. Sometimes you're even right. (Except to Mr. Buzzbottom. You're never right for his son, Buster.) Your choices can be as significant as how you'll deal with Sam's reading problems or as inconsequential as where to seat Buster today. Choices will include how you'll react to Darby when he tells on Buster for the 35th time before lunch, what color chalk you'll use, how much math you'll assign, and how you will let your Gospel light shine even on those kids hiding under bushel baskets. All those choices are an outgrowth of one earlier choice—the choice to become a teacher.

Not that you made that choice alone! No, God blessed that decision. Perhaps He even made it for you. Be assured that God always makes good choices. That's true even if teaching is difficult for you, even if your teaching career is coming to a premature or dissatisfying end. (If you find yourself in such a situation, God may be setting you up for a different ministry, one through which He can better use you.)

Today's Bible passage reports a portion of Solomon's now famous prayer. His life was about to be complicated with urgent and vital choices. He would decide cases of dispute and the course of a nation. Apparently, Solomon was concerned about making the correct choices. Because people would bow to his authority and seek his help, Solomon went to his Superior for assistance. He asked God to guide his choices.

Solomon's example is a good one to follow. Sin definitely will try to influence choices. Sometimes sin makes the wrong choices attractive or at least easy. You'll want to choose anger instead of tolerance when Buster acts like his dad. You may choose a cold shoulder over a warm heart toward a colleague who repeatedly hurts your feelings. The devil will tempt you to take the easy route in teaching the faith (facts alone instead of facts embedded in Christian relationships). Oh, temptations will accompany nearly every choice. So pray. Here's a good choice.

Prayer

Give Your servant a discerning heart to govern Your children and to distinguish between right and wrong. For who is able to govern these great students of Yours? Amen.

Better Red Than Dead

> O my God, I am too ashamed and disgraced to lift up my face to You, my God, because our sins are higher than our heads and our guilt has reached to the heavens. *Ezra 9:6*

Today's title would have resulted in no end of trouble for the publisher and writer had it appeared in the 1950s or 1960s. In those days, the slogan read, "Better dead than Red." It referred to the nation's fear of and aversion to communism. Today's title, however, reflects a spiritual reality: It's better to be red-faced embarrassed over our sins than to be dead in them.

Have you ever thought of how much redder faces would be if people could read minds? That consideration may help us place Ezra's prayer in context. His embarrassment resulted from the practices of God's people. God had shown them mercy while they were slaves of a foreign ruler. Instead of grateful obedience to God, however, the priests who served Him flouted God's Law in His face. Ezra's estimation of sin's extent was accurate. How embarrassing! He didn't even want to face heaven in prayer.

Sin easily reaches epic proportions—heaped to the heavens, as Ezra might say. We live in the shadows and gloom of that heap, and heaven's light would be forever blocked from our sight had Jesus not trampled the heap to dust. He buried our sins and left them in the grave that He vacated. Now when sin drives us to embarrassment, it's a good thing. We know how willingly and completely God forgives for Jesus' sake. As embarrassed as we may be over how blessed people like us could sin the way we do, God does not leave us to die. Thank God for revealing our guilt! Thank Jesus for taking it away! Thank the Spirit for helping us avoid future embarrassment!

You might want to end a school day by telling your class the story of Ezra, his people, and his prayer. Then you might conclude with his prayer. Remember one thing: Through Jesus Christ, God invites us to look up to Him. He will wipe the red from our faces.

Prayer

I'm embarrassed over my sins, Lord. How easily You catch me red-handed as well as red-faced! Please forgive me. Knowing that You have already answered my prayer, I look to You for strength and guidance. Amen.

Dismissal

"In My Father's house are many rooms; if it were not so, I would have told you. I am going there to prepare a place for you."

John 14:2

Isn't it strange how different emotional baggage accompanies the word *dismissal?* If the school board seeks dismissal of a teacher, they're not talking about the three o'clock bell. It's much the same for students. Their dismissal from school may come in the context of behavioral consequences or in the joy of going home after classes. Of course, we'll always have students whose dismissal at the end of the day carries with it the same dread as a more permanent dismissal. (Those students need a more loving and safe picture of home to understand a verse like today's. Those students need you to tell them more about their future home with Jesus.)

Under favorable circumstances, *home* has a positive connotation. It's a place where you don't need to subdue a yawn or muffle a loud laugh. It's a place you can say anything you please (because no one will pay attention to you anyway). Well, maybe that's going too far. Home is a place like no other. You probably have several homes. One may be where you came from. That home is mostly memories now, isn't it? Then there is your present home. Now there's some reality! You might also believe that your school sometimes feels like home, especially if you spend lots of time there. (Just be glad you don't have to buy shoes for all those kids!) Finally, there is the home to which you'll move for eternity. (Few Christians are in any great hurry to get there, but we all look forward to it!)

You are home right now. God wanted you to live and work here. He wanted you to establish Christian relationships and to teach others about the way to salvation. God wanted a place for you to relax and rest so you could spend productive time laboring for Christ, planting the seeds of faith given you by the Holy Spirit. Because God wanted your home to be the best, He sent His Son to live in your heart. That must be why the old cliché still has value: "Home is where the heart is."

Prayer

You have given me a lovely home, Lord. Thank You. Please live with my students, too, especially those who lack good earthly homes. Let them see the room in that mansion that You've prepared for them. Amen.

Noise

May those who delight in my vindication shout for joy and gladness; may they always say, "The LORD be exalted, who delights in the well-being of His servant." *Psalm 35:27*

Noise has gradually reached higher levels of acceptance in education. At one time, noise was considered as natural an academic enemy as sloth. Now some educational strategies even encourage noise. Some noise remains unacceptable, however. You may be one of those teachers who actually likes noise. If so, you should take up tennis. It's one sport where you always need to raise a racket. (Hey! You haven't groaned for several devotions now.)

Education has come to accept what the general public has known for years. Some noise is good while others is bad. Life is often cluttered with noise, but few would agree on which noises are pleasant and which are offensive. Noise offers some spiritual comparisons, but here the relative values of noise are far more clear.

First, there is the noise of sin. It's like soft rock in the ears of heavy metal fans or a polka to an afficionado of Gregorian chant. Sin is a noise that prevents enjoyment of God's Word or even blasts it into muteness. Worse yet, sin's noise may be more a dull, monotonous din—like the sound of a window air conditioner. It covers more useful and pleasant sounds without having a describable one of its own.

Second, there is the noise of salvation. You might associate it with the trumpets booked for the last day. It also can be a lullaby, triumphant march, or gavotte. (Look it up; it will only take a minuet. Was that *two* groans in one devotion?) Salvation's noise is always welcome and always joyful. It's a noise we may expect to hear from angels celebrating what the Savior did for you. It's the noise of the Lord Himself, applauding the victory He won for you on the cross.

You don't need a psalm or a rock band to make a little God-pleasing noise to the Lord. Even a whisper will do. Try it now.

Prayer

Praise to You, dear Savior! I can shout my praise even in silent prayer. May I join with my family, friends, colleagues, and students in a whooping worship of You for Your love and mercy toward us. Amen.

God Judgment

The LORD is known by His justice; the wicked are ensnared by the work of their hands.

Psalm 9:16

No, the title doesn't contain a typo. How much better than good can you get beyond God? God's justice is the only kind that is just plain just. While we don't know much about good judgment in our society, we do know that you can't expect good judgment because you hire more judges. Many modern rulings seem a step forward in liberty while pushing us farther back in God judgment.

Let's spend a couple of paragraphs judging judgment. First, let's agree that for anyone other than our Lord, snap judgments are undesirable. They become unsnapped so easily, exposing the kind of judgment we should have had in the first place. Maybe that's happened when you reacted angrily toward a student who arrived late for school. Again! Then you learned he was late because the newspaper delivery truck ran over his dog.

Second, we have the poor judgment scenario—or so it seems. Perhaps you've experienced that whining, tattle-tale, squeaky-voiced girl who spends every moment of recess annoying you with stories about other kids, siblings, parents, and pets. You might question her judgment. Be careful. Look whom she spends her time with at recess.

Third, we have the case of judging the future by the past. This brings tangible trouble! It takes us to today's psalm. The fairest judge in the universe has more than ample evidence to convict us and hand down a capital sentence. You're not wicked, you say? Perhaps by most standards you are far from wicked, but as God judges sin and sinners, you have no defense. Like today's jails, hell would be overcrowded were it not for another God judgment.

God sent Jesus to serve your sentence and expunge your record. Not you alone, of course. His lifesaving judgment extends to all who believe. Because God judges us in light of what Jesus did, heaven will have a full house. God judgment is indeed good—so good that someday we'll never live with the litter of bad judgments again.

Prayer

How good You are, God. You sent Your Son to take the punishment for my sins. Give me the same sort of merciful God judgment as I serve Your children as their teacher. Amen.

Safe Schools

The LORD will keep
you from all harm—He
will watch over your
life; the LORD will
watch over your com-
ing and going both now
and forevermore.

Psalm 121:7–8

Safety wasn't much of an issue in schools of yore. (Maybe yore school was an exception!) In those days, people discussed safety in terms of Ralph Nader and automobile safety. We probably would solve automobile problems more effectively if we recalled all the defective drivers rather than their vehicles! Either that or created cars that automatically locked the keys inside. But there is a more serious side to safety.

Safe schools are high on the list of what most parents want for their children. The intensity of that goal increases with every violent incident reported by the news media. Parents often perceive Christian schools as more safe than their public counterparts. In general, they usually do have a better record. But that's only partly true. You see, Christian schools can be the playground of Satan too.

While the devil romps freely wherever he is welcome (which is most everywhere), he especially enjoys infiltrating places frequented by Christians, budding ones in particular. (If you need proof of this, visit a church meeting at budget time or when a group is angry with the pastor or a teacher.) Christian schools and Christian teachers are favorite targets. If the devil can win you over, the victory is so much sweeter, probably as good as the one he enjoyed with Judas. Therefore, inhabitants of Christian schools encounter the persistent violence of spiritual warfare.

Not a good advertisement for Christian educational environments, is it? Of course, this is only half the story—the bad half. The truth is that despite the constant warfare, Christian teachers and their schools offer a safe haven from Satan. It's not really what the school does. It's what God has done that makes schools safe. By sending His Son to die a violent death for our sins, God made it safe for Christians to live happy and productive lives in the safety of salvation.

Prayer

Lord, keep me and my students safe. We surely need safety as we come and go—the kind You promise in today's psalm. But we also want safety from the devil and his evil designs on our lives. Amen.

Thinking Big

How precious to me are Your thoughts, O God! How vast is the sum of them!

Psalm 139:17

Two kinds of students occupy most classrooms. There are the thinking students and the Thing King students. You may be as familiar with the latter as you are with the former. The Thing Kings are collectors. Inspect their desks, and you'll unearth their treasures. On second thought, you may want to check your immunization records before undertaking that adventure!

Of course, you most appreciate the thinking students. Educators emphasize the thinking process, but perhaps we overrate it. Some of the most serious thinking takes place only when people find themselves bankrupt, hospitalized, jailed, or confronted by a demanding teacher.

If you value thinkers and thinking, then you'll appreciate today's psalm. As you reflect on God's power and mercy, the wonder of it might dwarf your thoughts. Just what does God think? We can't begin to fathom the answer to that question because we are limited by our skimpy, human thinking. Let's exercise what little we have anyway.

God thinks big. He didn't create just a street or a subdivision. He put together an entire universe and everything necessary to sustain it. God didn't stop with plants and animals. He saved His best efforts for humans. He created us in His image and gave us the power to think. From a human perspective, that was a mistake because the first two humans thought they should know more than they did. You would think that God would condemn the inventors of worldly weakness, but He planned to save them and all the sinners to come.

God thinks you're a good person. Oh, you're not fooling Him. His thinking is too perfect for that. God not only thinks you're a good person, He knows it! He sent Jesus to take away your sins just as He promised Adam and Eve He would do. God thinks of you often—every moment, in fact. His thinking keeps you a faithful servant. His thinking protects you from sin and other evil. You can read more about what God thinks. Just open the Bible. Consider it His version of a "Thinking of You" card.

Prayer

Dear God, thank You for thinking of me—for making me a believer and giving me an important ministry by which I can serve You. Amen.

Fountain of Knowledge

Jesus answered, "My teaching is not My own. It comes from Him who sent Me." *John 7:16*

Colleagues asked a retiring teacher to leave them with some words of wisdom. She responded, "Remember this: There are students who drink deeply at the fountain of knowledge while others just gargle."

Students believe they know a lot. But batting averages, rock star tours, computer games, and the latest toy fads aren't really that important in the scheme of life. (Don't try to convince them, though, that anything else is more important!)

As an educator, your life is soaked with knowledge. Maybe *soaked* is a poor word choice. Your students probably think you're all wet. You would be in good company, however, because Jesus faced the same suspicion. In the verse preceding today's Bible passage, we find the context for Jesus' comment. "The Jews were amazed and asked, 'How did this man get such learning without having studied?'" (John 7:15). Now you might expect this question if a student notorious for academic lethargy got an *A* on his report card, but to ask it about Jesus reflected serious misunderstanding. The Jews didn't accept Him as God's Son. Had Jesus been a cocky young man, He might have said, "Do you know who I am?" But notice how His answer is both wise and humble. Jesus merely cited the source of His knowledge—a verbal footnote to His teaching.

Have you experienced students who think that you know everything because you are a teacher? (At least students agree with you at some point in their academic lives!) As students age, they become more skeptical (or realistic). Therefore, it's wise to specify the source of your treasure trove of knowledge, especially your knowledge of salvation.

Whatever you know about God comes from the Bible, of course. But there is more to it. You believe the Bible! Your faith comes from the same place the Bible originated. Both are God's gifts. Everything you know about sin and your need for salvation came from the only impeccable source of knowledge worth knowing—God Himself. That's one footnote that belongs at the top of the page!

Prayer

Heavenly Father, thank You for the living Word as well as for the words I read in the Bible. Without them, I would be terminally ignorant. Thank You for sending the Holy Spirit to bring the Bible to life within me. Amen.

A Good Sign

This will be a sign to you: You will find a baby wrapped in cloths and lying in a manger.
Luke 2:12

If you were allowed to post any sign on your school's property, what would it say? Where would you place the sign? Would it qualify as Law or Gospel?

One public school displayed an interesting sign on its campus. The sign read: "No one allowed on school property during the school day." Can you imagine the possible outcomes of obedience to this edict? The truancy officer says, "Ma'am, why isn't your child in school?" You can fill in the blanks with the answer.

The best sign ever was recorded in today's Bible verse. Maybe we should post signs with that illustration around our schools. Imagine its impact on passersby, as opposed to signs such as "You will be incarcerated for 99 years if you enter this school without a permit!" Perhaps you can think of other signs that would tell the public the mission of your school. Sounds like a good project for the parent group. Or the art class.

Over time, you become accustomed to signs. Perhaps seeing the same ones in the same places finally dulls you to their messages. Think for a moment of the signs located near your school. What are they? Can you remember?

Is the sign Luke talks about in danger of fading into the background because you and your students are routinely exposed to it? Pray that it doesn't because what greater joy is there than to hear this Good News. It's the same Good News message that has been shared for more than 2,000 years! It hasn't lost any of the luster from the original angel-communicated proclamation. Who could ever improve on this old story?

The longer you are a Christian, the more you rejoice in the basic sign of God's love—Jesus lying in the manger. It's easy to get caught up in more complex spiritual matters, relegating Jesus in the manger to December's bulletin board. But never forget about God coming to earth as Man. And if your focus strays, don't let it stray farther than the empty tomb.

Prayer

Father, who am I that You would announce the Savior's birth to me again and again? Thank You for sending the Savior to me. Thank You for all the reminders of Your love for me. Amen.

Goals and Objectives

Were there ever two words more familiar to a teacher's vocabulary? Goals and objectives! They permeate curriculum sometimes to the extent that you no longer want to hear them. They give direction and help define success. Goals and objectives are serious tools for learning. But education isn't the only environment anxious to establish goals and objectives. They drive commerce and industry too. Where money is to be made or lost, goals and objectives are serious business. On the flip side, if you aim at nothing, you're sure to hit it!

Are you so foolish? After beginning with the Spirit, are you now trying to attain your goal by human effort?

Galatians 3:3

The general public has goals. With a little help, usually from a credit company, people often reach them. The key here is "help," which brings us to Paul's words in today's Bible passage. Reaching our goal as Christians requires outside help. Among the many temptations

Christians face, one of the biggest is losing focus. It happens when we find ourselves caught up in good works and obedience and we overlook the Spirit's scope and sequence.

Why do we help? You know the answer, and not because you're a teacher. We need help because we are sinners, unable to produce any good work. Only through the saving work of Jesus can we reach the final goal of eternal life in His presence and the intermediate goals of serving Him and bringing glory to God. That brings us to a few more words from the Bible: "Though you have not seen Him, you love Him; and even though you do not see Him now, you believe in Him and are filled with an inexpressible and glorious joy, for you are receiving the goal of your faith, the salvation of your souls" (1 Peter 1:8–9).

While most goals and objectives are observable, the object of our goal as Christians cannot be seen. For now, it's enough to love Jesus and enjoy His company on a spiritual level. Notice that the goal is already accomplished! So enjoy yourself.

Prayer

Keep me goal oriented, dear Jesus. Help me live my life in ways that show how You accomplished the goal for me. Never let me give credit to anyone but You. Amen.

Laughter's Medicine

But You, O LORD, laugh at them; You scoff at all those nations. *Psalm 59:8*

An old proverb says: "He who laughs last probably has loose false teeth." That's about as funny as this one gets. A word search of the Bible reveals little laughter—no "hee haws" or "ho hos." This doesn't mean that God's people didn't laugh nor does it preclude a disciple with a sense of humor. It doesn't prevent you from exercising your sense of humor in the class-room. In fact, religion class might benefit from a little light-heartedness that reflects the joy of our salvation. We can assume that with all the joy and rejoicing mentioned in God's Word, believers laughed frequently.

God's laughter in today's Bible verse isn't joyful—it's derisive. This was David's psalm composed when Saul's hit men were looking for him. David trusted God's plans for him, but he also asked for help. In doing so, he reviewed God's power. David knew that God could laugh scornfully at the strongest of leaders and armies because He was King of kings, Lord of lords, hallelujah! (David had a good Handel on that concept.)

The main reason modern Christians can laugh is that God remains King of kings. His power enables us to laugh in contempt of our worst enemy, the devil. As you know, laughing at enemies can be dangerous, especially when they're powerful and malicious. But by God's power through Jesus' living, dying, and rising, the devil's potential is limited. Even if he deprives you of earthly life, he can never filch the immortality won for you by Jesus.

Laughter facilitates healing. You've probably noticed how a good joke or humorous remark can break the tension in a classroom or at a faculty meeting. Laughter can have the same effect as you review your salvation. So much threatens to stand in the way of happiness—sinful rebelliousness against God, for example. But thanks be to God, the joy of Jesus remains in your heart. Go ahead, laugh.

Prayer

Thank You, Lord, for defeating the devil. Now I can laugh like David. Better yet, keep the joy of Jesus in my heart—and place some of it on my face too. Amen.

Final Exam

Examine yourselves to see whether you are in the faith; test yourselves. Do you not realize that Christ Jesus is in you?

2 Corinthians 13:5

You have almost completed *Teaching 201.* When you complete something in school, it's time to examine yourself. It's time for the dreaded final exam.

The second sentence makes this sound like a lenient test. Examine yourself? What student wouldn't tingle with delight at that prospect? On the other hand, maybe it's more difficult than it sounds. Self-examination can take two courses. There's the easy way: one question, true or false. Of course when you think it's a cinch to ace the test, sooner or later the problems come. Sooner—when you realize you're fooling yourself. And later—when you are expected to apply what you know.

The second course for this self-examination is equally as bad. When you look at yourself, you might be an extra-critical judge. No matter what you know, how well you know it, what you can do, or how well you can do it, it's never enough to satisfy you.

Having examined the phrase "examine yourself" and finding the process more difficult than it appears, let's see what Paul wanted to assess. He wanted to "see whether you are in the faith." Sounds serious, doesn't it? In fact, your life depends on your answer.

What's the best way to examine yourself for faith? If you examine yourself according to the first course, the answer is an automatic yes, no further thought necessary. But what about those late-night nagging doubts? Taking the second course might find you comparing and contrasting the good you have done with the bad you have done divided by all the things you should have done but didn't do. The answer might prod you to try harder, but the harder you try, the more you perceive your deficiencies. Woe is you!

Paul, being the good teacher he was, would sympathize with your dilemma. In fact, he shamelessly recorded his own examination in Romans 7. But in Romans 5:1–2 Paul answered the question of whether you are in faith. Here's the answer word for Word: "Therefore, since we have been justified through faith, we have peace with God through our Lord Jesus Christ through whom we have gained access by faith into this grace in which we now stand. And we rejoice in the hope of the glory of God." Paul got that answer from Someone—the same Someone who still hasn't retired from teaching His children!

Prayer

Amen. Praise to You, dear Lord. Amen.

Reviving the Romance

As a young man marries a maiden, so will your sons marry you; as a bridegroom rejoices over his bride, so will your God rejoice over you. *Isaiah 62:5*

Someone once said, "A romance that begins by a babbling brook sometimes ends over (or under) a leaky sink." Not so with you. Your marriage was made in heaven. You're still the bride, and He is still the bridegroom. Of course, this isn't a gender thing. The Bible uses bridegroom/bride language in several places. The Bridegroom is Jesus and you are the bride.

Talk about a twinkle in the Bridegroom's eye! You were always His dream. His romance culminated on the cross where He died. How tragic if the love story ended there! But Easter dawned on an eternal honeymoon.

Love breeds love. The more it is given, the more it grows. So it is with Jesus and you. But like human marriage, spiritual marriage takes work—if you can call it that. Work may seem drudgery, undignified, or boringly routine when performed outside the realm of romance. But just as newlyweds joyfully labor in love, Jesus and you work happily for each other.

Make no mistake. This marriage was Jesus' idea. Through His sacrifice for you—and the matchmaking of the Holy Spirit—you came to know Him. He wrote a long love letter to you, and by the power of the Spirit, you believed every word. Now you're together, and you work for Him.

As inappropriate as it seems in American culture, your Bridegroom chose your life's work. Even more surprisingly, you're probably honored to do it. What a privilege to teach children! True, God chose many people for this task, but your role stretches beyond consonant blends, higher-level math, molecules, and jumping jacks. Your job includes telling students about your marriage.

As you complete this book, think about reviving your romance with Jesus. Don't keep His love letters bundled in the back of a drawer. Read them again and again. Think about the children you serve and how He has empowered you to teach them. Then as you finish this book, think of this: "The bride belongs to the bridegroom. The friend who attends the bridegroom waits and listens for him, and is full of joy when he hears the bridegroom's voice. That joy is mine, and it is now complete" (John 3:29).

Prayer

Lord Jesus, thank You for making me Your own. Although undeserving, You chose to save me. In praise and thanksgiving, I ask You to empower me to do whatever You desire of me. Keep me faithful to You. Let our honeymoon never end. Amen.

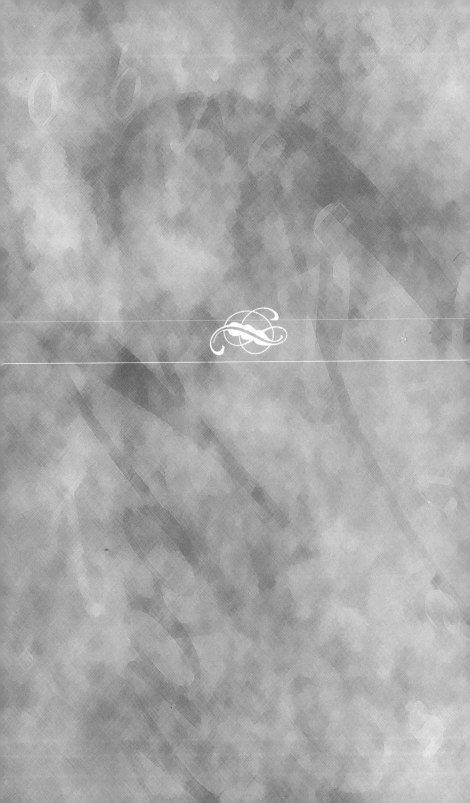